FLORA IN FOCUS

# BOTANICAL GARDENS

SMITHMARK

For this English language edition:
Todtri Productions Ltd., New York

This edition published in 1996 by SMITHMARK
Publishers, a division of U.S. Media Holdings,
Inc., 16 East 32nd Street, New York, NY 10016.

SMITHMARK books are available for bulk pur-
chase for sales promotion and premium use. For
details write or call the manager of special sales,
SMITHMARK Publishers, 16 East 32nd Street,
New York, NY 10016; (212) 532-6600.

Editions of this book will appear simultaneously
in France, Germany, Great Britain, Italy and
the Netherlands under auspices of Euredition bv,
Den Haag, Netherlands

*Photographs:*
PPWW Plant Pictures World Wide, Daan Smit
*Text:*
Nicky den Hartogh
*Translation:*
Tony Langham
*Concept, design and editing:*
Boris van Dobbenburgh
*Typesetting:*
Mark Dolk/Peter Verwey Grafische Produkties
*Color separation:*
Unifoto PTY LTD, Cape Town
*Production:*
Agora United Graphic Services bv, 's-Graveland
*Printing and binding:*
Egedsa, Sabadell, Spain

ISBN 0-8317-6119-9

# INTRODUCTION

Since the end of the seventeenth century, exotic plants have been imported into Europe on a large scale. The most powerful countries of the past equipped sailing vessels to colonize territories overseas, and trade in spices and other products from distant countries. Trading companies brought back seeds, important commercial crops and exotic ornamental plants. Rulers and powerful merchants sent botanists to every corner of the world. Botanical gardens flourished because of the hitherto unknown wealth of plants from the American, Australian, African and Asian continents.

Before that time, botanical gardens specialized mainly in the cultivation and study of medicinal herbs. They served medical science, primarily for the acquisition of knowledge about the effects and uses of medicinal plants. In most cases they were part of the universities in particular towns. Prospective physicians and pharmacists were taught by studying the plants. The first botanical gardens were established in rapid succession in the Italian cities of Pisa (1543), Padua (1545), and Florence (1550). These were followed by gardens in cities in Northern Europe, including Leiden (1587), Paris (1635), Amsterdam (1638) and Edinburgh (1670).

When the importance of science increased towards the end of the Middle Ages, there was also a growing interest in nature. The study of plants was no longer concerned only with their usefulness to man, but also with the composition of plants, flowers, fruits and seeds. A systematic classification was drawn up of the vegetable kingdom, based on similarities and differences. As botany covered an increasingly broad field, striking developments took place in botanical gardens.
The study of plants is known as botany (botanica). "Hortus" means garden. This is why a garden aimed at the scientific study of plants may be known as a hortus botanicus, or botanical garden.

Botanical gardens were not only concerned with research and educational matters, but have also played an important role through the centuries with regard to the collection and spread of plants. Famous botanical gardens such as those in St. Petersburg, Kew Gardens in London and the Jardin des Plantes in Paris sent representatives to unexplored regions to discover, describe and collect unknown plants.

To do this, the botanists had to overcome the greatest imaginable dangers, and sometimes paid for their courage with their lives.
In America, missionaries were often called upon to be botanists. All sorts of plants were brought to Europe from China and Japan, countries which had a highly developed garden culture, but had been cut off from the outside world in the West for a long time. They were brought back by the French priest, d'Incarville, and the German-Dutch doctor and botanist, Von Siebold. They were able to make the necessary contacts because they had technical skills which were needed in the countries concerned.

As Europe fell ever more deeply under the spell of the exotic wonders of nature, there was an increasing need for better places to cultivate the new plants. The orangeries, where subtropical plants such as citrus trees (orange trees), laurel, myrtle and oleander were wintered in tubs, were too dark for plants from the tropics. In the course of the eighteenth century the buildings started to incorporate more and more glass, and gradually they began to look more and more like real conservatories. The Palm House in the botanical gardens at Kew was finished in 1848. This is a magnificent example of Victorian architecture in glass, with elegant wrought-iron arches, graceful spiral staircases, slender pillars, and ornamental balustrades. The building was tall enough to accommodate palms and other large tropical plants. The botanical gardens of Copenhagen and Florence also built impressive palm houses.
The Royal Botanic Gardens in Kew were the first to have a Victoria conservatory, where the giant waterlily from the Amazon Basin of South America was exhibited. This stunning water plant, with its floating leaves with a diameter of six feet, was described and drawn in the year of the coronation of Queen Victoria, and thereby named Victoria regia. The pool, with the flowering Victoria regia (later known as Victoria amazonica) became one of the most popular public attractions.

The fascination with exotic plants did not confine itself to botanical gardens. Rulers, statesmen and rich merchants also established private collections of plants. The trade in exotic plants expanded enormously, and eventually endangered the survival of several varieties of plants in their countries of origin. The first botanical gardens in the overseas territories themselves were established in the eighteenth and nineteenth centuries. Most of these were originally aimed at scientific research into the cultivation and production methods of economically valuable plants. Some of these gardens, such as the botanical gardens in Bogor, on Java (Indonesia), not only expanded to become important scientific centers in the field of tropical botany, but also played a significant role in the conservation of the indigenous flora of the country concerned.

The past can live on in a botanical garden where the oldest palm ferns, the tallest palm trees, and the most awe-inspiring trees are exhibited. Their history dates back through centuries and it is particularly the stories about the origins and possible uses of plants that continue to arouse interest. Time and time again the fragrance of Victoria amazonica in the first night that it flowers is one of the greatest attractions, and the short-lived beauty of the flowering Queen of Night (Selenicereus grandiflorus) is a high point in the life of a botanical garden. As science has increasingly depended on research carried out in laboratories, there has been a great decline in the importance of botanical gardens for scientific research in the last few decades. On the other hand, public interest in indigenous flora, as well as in plants from other parts of the world, is constantly growing. In that respect, botanical gardens are very interesting places. The plants are no longer arranged by definition, in accordance with the families to which they are related, as they were in earlier gardens which were arranged according to classifications, but may be laid out in accordance with their geographical points of correspondence. This means that in many botanical gardens, charming miniature landscapes have been created where it is possible to enjoy a stroll without directly feeling any need to be informed. In the conservatories one can enter little areas of rainforest, desert or misty mountain forests. A full-color brochure for a Swedish garden invites prospective visitors to "travel the world in an hour. Start in Asia !" Although an hour is very short, and the comparison with a trip around the world seems rather ambitious, it is possible to be something of an explorer in a botanical garden. The smell of the earth, the flowering jasmine, the subtropical herbs and humid tropical heat all contribute to the image of the plant world in distant lands.

Nowadays, seeds and plants are exchanged between botanical gardens wherever possible, but at the same time each botanical garden tries to specialize in a particular field. Some may collect as many insectivores as possible (insect-eating plants), while others have extensive collections of orchids. Throughout the world botanical gardens are working intently to cross-fertilize varieties which have nearly become extinct, and to cultivate new varieties. The study and conservation of threatened species has become one of the most important tasks of modern botanical gardens.

C ARLOS THAYS BOTANICAL GARDENS, BUENOS AIRES
Tropical water-lily.

NATIONAL BOTANICAL GARDENS OF BELGIUM, MEISE
In 1826 a botanical garden was founded in the capital of Belgium. It was taken over by the State in 1870 and expanded to become an important scientific center with an impressive complex of conservatories. When it became clear that there was no room for further expansion, the estate of Bouchout in Meise, near Brussels, was chosen for the new site of the botanical gardens. The estate is landscaped in the English style, and covers 230 acres. There is an old castle where the Empress Charlotte, wife of Maximilian of Mexico, lived until 1927. The center of the National Botanical Gardens of Belgium, as it has been known since 1967, is the Palace of Plants. Its construction started in 1947. The Palace consists of thirteen large exhibition conservatories, of which twelve are open to the public. They form a rectangle, enclosing smaller conservatories with special collections. The latter, like the central large conservatory, are open only to "specialists and collectors." Most of the public conservatories are devoted to the flora of particular regions. For example, the two conservatories of African plants contain, among others, the umbrella tree (Musanga cecropioides) from the African rainforest, the beautiful Traveler's tree (Ravenala madagascariensis) from Madagascar, and the strangely shaped screw pine. (Pandanus utilis). The dome-shaped former Victoria conservatory (photograph) is no longer used. The tropical water plants, including Victoria amazonica and Victoria cruziana, now grow in a pool in the Palace of Plants.

BOTANICAL GARDENS OF THE UNIVERSITY OF GHENT
Since 1900 the botanical gardens of the University of Ghent have been in the center of the city. The most beautiful part is probably the Victoria conservatory. This contains a large rectangular pool surrounded by luxuriant vegetation consisting of tropical plants. Here and there, enormous cheese plants (Monstera deliciosa) grow up to the ridge. In summer the large leaves of Victoria amazonica and Victoria cruziana float on the water and various different water-lilies flower (Victoria conservatory). ▶

## BOTANICAL GARDENS OF THE UNIVERSITY OF COPENHAGEN

The magnificent palm house complex of the botanical gardens in Copenhagen (Denmark) is a striking example of monumental nineteenth-century glass architecture. It was built between 1872 and 1874, and has not lost its original glory after more than a hundred years.

## BOTANICAL GARDENS OF THE UNIVERSITY OF COPENHAGEN

Palm house with bust of Frederik V by the side of the Victoria pool. During the reign of this Danish king (1746-1766), the country experienced a period of unbroken peace, and trade, the sciences and the arts flourished.

# BOTANICAL GARDENS OF THE UNIVERSITY OF COPENHAGEN

Visitors get an impression of the atmosphere in humid tropical regions in the domed palm house in Copenhagen, which is fifty feet high. The center is formed by the ancient and enormous Livistona rotundifolia, of which the top reaches the top of the glass dome. This fan palm was cultivated long ago from the seed of a specimen in the celebrated botanical gardens, Buitenzorg (later known as Kebun Raya) in Bogor on Java. The "Cape plants," which are moved into the conservatory complex for the winter, include specimens which are more than a hundred years

old, such as the mastic tree (Pistacia lenticus), and the Cyprus turpentine (Pistacia terebinthus).

As in many other botanical gardens, the area with cash crops - which include coffee, tea, banana, and many members of the citrus family (lemons, grapefruit, oranges etc.) - attracts a great deal of public interest all year round. The botanical gardens of Copenhagen focus special attention on high alpine and polar plants, which are not easy to cultivate because they require a cold environment and have specific requirements regarding their location.

BOTANICAL GARDENS OF THE UNIVERSITY OF COPENHAGEN
Flower of a tropical water-lily hybrid: Nymphaea "Director G.T. Moore"

# BOTANICAL GARDENS OF THE UNIVERSITY OF COPENHAGEN

The giant water-lily with its enormous floating leaves and charming flowers was discovered in the Amazon basin at the beginning of the nineteenth century. When we say "discovered," we mean discovered by a European. The Indians who lived by the river had known the plant since time immemorial, and ate its seeds after roasting them. In 1837, the year in which Queen Victoria was crowned, the "Queen of the Amazon" was given the name Victoria. For a long time the plant was known as Victoria regia, but nowadays its official name is Victoria amazonica. In 1849, botanists finally succeeded in getting a seedling to flower in the famous botanical gardens of Kew (London). Henceforth, all self-respecting botanical gardens did everything they could to show the public a flowering "Vic." Herrenhausen near

Hannover succeeded in 1851, followed by the Amsterdam botanical gardens, "De Plantage," in 1859. Special Victoria conservatories appeared everywhere, often just as elegant as the plant itself. Newspapers and brochures published the date when the night-flowering "Vic" would unfold its fragrant flowers, and the evening hours at which the botanical gardens would be open to exhibit the miracle. The plant was a special attraction for children, who could be seated on the enormously strong leaves which could be up to six feet in diameter. Victoria cruziana is cultivated in the Victoria pool of the botanical gardens in Copenhagen. This is also a majestic water plant, though the leaves are slightly smaller and have higher edges than those of Victoria amazonica.

# BOTANICAL GARDENS AND BOTANICAL MUSEUM, BERLIN-DAHLEM, BERLIN

The botanical gardens in Berlin are among the most interesting in Europe. They were established in Berlin-Dahlem in 1897, but their history goes back to 1646, when the original garden was founded. From the beginning of the nineteenth century, the botanical gardens of Berlin distinguished themselves in the field of the geography of plants as a result of the work of Karl Ludwig Willdenow. After being destroyed in the Second World War, the botanical gardens were rebuilt on the ruins of the former garden. Again a great deal of attention was focused on the geography of plants: a large number of areas were created in miniature, clearly demonstrating the characteristic vegetation of different types of landscapes throughout the world, varying from steppes to alpine regions. The botanical gardens comprise a museum and seventy-five conservatories, including a conservatory of succulents with an extensive collection of cacti.

# GRUGAPARK AND THE BOTANICAL GARDENS OF ESSEN

Part of the rock garden, with a background of conifers. The botanical gardens of the city of Essen in Germany are part of the spectacular Grugapark. The park has an area of 170 acres and has a strong emphasis on recreation. The orangery consists of three pavilions, and devotes attention to art and culture, as well as subtropical plants. The attractions for the public include a music hall, cafés and restaurants, an aviary for exotic birds, children's play areas, and a 165-foot-long geographical wall, which shows evolution on earth. In the rock garden with primulas,

saxifrage, gentian and edelweiss, there is a high rock formation from which a mountain brook cascades down. The complex of conservatories consists of a number of large and small glass pyramids. In the largest there are collections of plants from the tropical rainforest, such as Monstera, Heliconia, Philodendron, Anthurium, and Dracaena. In the conservatory which is devoted to subtropical misty mountain forests there are large tree ferns and many species of bromelia and other ferns.

# THE PALM GARDEN IN FRANKFURT

The German architect, Hermann Blomeier, succeeded in continuing the tradition of the great nineteenth century designers with the "Tropicarium," the new conservatory in the Palm Garden in Frankfurt, although the building is very different from the Victorian conservatories, for example, at Kew Gardens or Copenhagen. The Tropicarium was completed in 1987. The architect got the idea for the characteristic star shape, which can be recognized in the large and small areas of the conservatory complex, when he saw a cross section of the Cereus cactus. The computer system which regulates the climatic conditions in the different areas of the complex is connected to the meteorological station in Frankfurt, so that the temperature can be directly regulated according to the weather.

◄ GRUGAPARK AND THE BOTANICAL
GARDENS OF ESSEN
Interior of a conservatory.

THE PALM GARDEN IN FRANKFURT
The Palm Garden in Frankfurt has an extensive collection of plants.
Tropical and subtropical flora from many different regions are represented in large numbers. The cactus collection consists of more than 1,500 species, not only the indisputable desert plants, but also epiphytic cacti which live in trees in misty forests, such as Rhipsalis and Epiphyllum. The Palm Garden serves not only as a botanical garden with an area of fifty acres, but is also designed for recreation. Visitors can enjoy special exhibitions and musical performances, particularly in summer.

# BOTANICAL GARDENS OF JUSTUS LIEBIG UNIVERSITY, GIESSEN

A flowering summer border in the botanical gardens in the German city of Giessen. These botanical gardens, part of Justus Liebig University, date from the beginning of the seventeenth century. There are fifteen conservatories in the limited space of ten acres, housing, amongst other things, a collection of epiphytes: plants which live on the trunks and branches of trees, extracting food from the air and rotting detritus. Borders with annuals, perennials, alpine plants and plants from the Steppes have been planted in the open air outside the conservatory. Part of the garden is devoted to medicinal and toxic plants.

## BOTANICAL GARDENS OF THE UNIVERSITY OF HAMBURG

A conservatory of succulents in the old garden.

## BOTANICAL GARDENS OF THE UNIVERSITY OF HAMBURG

The profusely flowering bright pink "color fountain," Cleome hassleriana "Cerise Queen," surrounded by other annual plants in the summer border of the old botanical gardens in Hamburg. Cleome owes its name, "color fountain," to the stamens which protrude a long way outside the corolla.

# ROYAL GARDENS OF HERRENHAUSEN, HANNOVER

The botanical gardens in Hannover form part of the Royal Gardens of Herrenhausen, the former summer residence of German rulers. The "Grosse Garten" was a splendid baroque garden dating from the seventeenth century. The adjacent "Berggarten" was once an orchard, and was gradually transformed into an unusual botanical garden with the planting of rare and valuable exotic plants. In the course of the eighteenth and nineteenth centuries, thirty-four orangeries and conservatories were built, and one of the most extensive collections of orchids at that time was exhibited

there. The first Victoria amazonica flowered on June 15, 1851. Almost thirty years later, a palm house was built, with a height of one hundred feet, making it the tallest in the world. When the entire Berggarten was destroyed in the Second World War, modern conservatories were built, and a new collection of plants was acquired. The Herrenhäuser Allee, which is more than one mile long and runs from Hannover to the garden complex, is bordered with lime trees.

# BOTANICAL GARDENS OF FRIEDRICH SCHILLER UNIVERSITY, JENA

The history of botanical gardens goes back to 1586 when a hortus medicus (medicinal garden) was established at the University of Jena for the students of the faculty of medicine. It was partly as a result of the efforts of the well-known poet and natural scientist, Goethe, that the present site was made available for botanical gardens in 1794. The garden grew to become a delightful place, popular with royal visitors. The small Goethe Museum in the former 'Inspector-Haus' is a reminder of the fact that Goethe stayed there from time to time to devote himself entirely to botanical research.

The botanical gardens have an area of almost twelve acres, and comprise, among other things, a rock garden (alpinum), containing rock plants and mountain plants from every continent. Special stones and mixtures of soil have been deposited there for the sensitive specimens among the mountain flora. For water plants there is an indoor and an outdoor pool. The large Victoria conservatory was built in 1968. Amongst the tropical water plants there are tubs with palm trees and papyrus. The magnificent high-edged leaves of Victoria regia and Victoria cruziana float in the water, and the delicate petals of Egyptian water-lilies and Indian lotus flowers spread everywhere. The Indian or sacred lotus (Nelumbo nucifera) comes from Asia. It is considered a sacred plant by Hindus and Buddhists. ▶

# BOTANICAL GARDENS OF FRIEDRICH SCHILLER UNIVERSITY, JENA

# BOTANICAL GARDENS OF WUPPERTAL

The orangeries of botanical gardens, which admit far less light than glass conservatories, are excellent for wintering succulent plants which require dry, cool, but frost-free conditions in winter. They do not require much light, because there is virtually no growth during the winter months. During this time they are given very little water. After a recovery period, these so-called "orangery" or tub plants (also known as "Cape plants") are usually placed outside the orangery as soon as the danger of frost has passed. Traditionally the curiously-shaped Agaves, Dracaenas, Furcraeas, and Yuccas - all members of the Agave family - have an important place amongst the tub plants which like dry conditions. Some members of the Agave family are armed with such ferocious thorns that it is by no means easy to transfer the pots or tubs. A tree-shaped yucca stands by the outside wall of the orangery in the small botanical gardens of Wuppertal.

# BOTANICAL GARDENS OF FRANKFURT

Yucca filamentosa is one of the few palm lilies which can grow in the open ground in the temperate regions of the northern hemisphere. Because of the elegant grace of the tall inflorescences and the decorative, sword-shaped leaves, the palm lily is a valuable acquisition for any botanical garden open to the public. There are approximately thirty other varieties of yucca. The majority of these originate in the dry regions of the southern United States and Central America. In cool European countries they are cultivated in conservatories for succulents and in orangeries. Further south, the plants enhance the gardens of villas, parks and botanical gardens.

# THE WILHELMA ZOOLOGICAL-BOTANICAL GARDENS, STUTTGART

In the Wilhelma zoological and botanical gardens in Stuttgart, the summer borders are strikingly colorful, and so much attention has been devoted to the arrangement of the tropical and subtropical plants that true landscapes have been created in the conservatories. Outside, the charming camellias and ancient magnolias with their large, tulip-shaped flowers create an overwhelming impression in spring. In the Moorish conservatories, the azaleas are in full bloom. The large Victoria pool is particularly worthwhile at the height of summer. The open-air pool is kept at the right temperature for the "Vic" and for tropical water-lilies by means of a heating system. Crocodiles, snakes, hummingbirds, pelicans, ostriches, turtles and many other animals in the zoological and botanical gardens live in a green world of tropical orchids, bromelias, heliconias and palm trees, creating a harmonious interaction of plant and animal life. (The garden was founded in 1853 and covers an area of sixty acres.)

## BOTANICAL GARDENS OF LYON
(Parc de la Tête d'Or)

The majority of the plants in the botanical gardens in Lyon are arranged on the basis of a geographic correspondence. The mountain plants from various areas have been brought together in an alpinum or rock garden, in which various stones and soils have been placed to approximate the environment in the regions where the plants originated as far as possible. The Cyclamen hederifolium shown here grows in lime-rich soil together with other lime-loving mountain plants.

## BOTANICAL GARDENS OF LYON
(Parc de la Tête d'Or)

The rich and varied collections of plants of the botanical gardens in the Parc de la Tête d'Or, Lyon, are internationally renowned. The many remarkable specimens of tropical flora include the swan flower (Aristolochia littoralis) from Brazil. Almost all year round the strange flowers peep out from the leaf axilla. The plant was first imported to France from South America in 1883.

# BOTANICAL GARDENS OF LYON
## (Parc de la Tête d'Or)

The large Parc de la Tête d'Or was opened in 1856 to enable the inhabitants of the French city of Lyon to spend their days off in a green area. It covers an area of 275 acres, and contains a large lake fed by the nearby river Rhône. A number of striking vantage points provide a view of the most beautiful parts of the area. Gradually the botanical gardens also developed. From 1877 to 1880 a series of conservatories were built, including the large conservatory for palms which accommodates plants from five different climatic regions.

# BOTANICAL GARDENS LES CÈDRES, ST.-JEAN-CAP-FERRAT

St.-Jean-Cap-Ferrat is on the coast of southern France, where subtropical plants flourish under the influence of the mild Mediterranean climate. Of the approximately 35 acres available for the botanical gardens of Les Cèdres, seven acres are devoted to the natural vegetation of the region. Two acres are is taken up by conservatories. These contain plants which have special requirements regarding temperature or humidity. Plants which like dry conditions, which come from the areas with little rainfall, strong sunshine and often searing winds, grow in the conservatory for succulents. They include succulent euphorbias, aloes, members of the agave family, the mesenbryanthemum family and the sedum family, in addition to columnar, and bushy, spherical cacti. The collection of succulents in Les Cèdres is one of the largest in the world.

# EXOTIC GARDENS AT VAL RAHMEN, MENTON

The villa "Val Rahmen" is situated in Menton in the south of France, near the Italian border. The house is built in a purely Provençal style and served as a winter residence in the past. Since 1950 an English lady has planted a botanical collection with a very exotic character in the terraced garden surrounding the villa. Colorful subtropical plants from different parts of the world are represented. The villa is situated in such an agreeable location that some of the decidedly heat-loving plants have acclimatized over the course of the years. The paradise-bird flowers (Strelitzia reginae) from southern Africa have developed particularly strikingly. The orange and blue flowers are like the crest of a cockatoo above the large boat-shaped bract (the "beak").

# JARDIN DES PLANTES, PARIS

As in many of the botanical gardens which are centuries old, the Jardin des Plantes in Paris developed from an apothecary's garden where medicinal herbs were cultivated. Part of the modern Jardin des Plantes is still governed by the austere layout of the past. This "formal garden" is divided by straight paths with rigidly edged flowerbeds on either side, in the fashion of the seventeenth century. Another part of the botanical gardens has a more natural character because the winding paths are more arbitrary and there are beautiful groups of trees. The cedar of Lebanon of Jussieu can be found there. This tree was imported to France in 1735 by Bernard Jussieu, a director who was able to import plants to Europe from China, which was virtually inaccessible at that time, with the intervention of the priest Pierre d'Incarville. The collections of alpine plants, succulents, Fuschia and Pelargonium are some of the specialist varieties of the botanical gardens in Paris. Apart from being a scientific center and botanical garden, the Jardin des Plantes is also important as a zoological garden, certainly for Parisians.

JARDIN DES PLANTES, PARIS

# BOTANICAL GARDENS OF THE VILLA TARANTO, PALLANZA

The Villa Taranto in Pallanza is situated in a magnificent Italian landscape on Lake Maggiore in northern Italy, near the Swiss border. The villa and the territory around it was bought in 1930 by an Englishman who created a botanical garden of great beauty with an expert trained at Kew Gardens. The garden was planned mainly in a landscape style. In spring all the attention is focused on the spectacular blossoming magnolias and Japanese ornamental cherry trees. In Italy the splendid borders of perennials - a typically English feature of garden art - are rather unusual. The lawn between the flower borders looks out over the "cherubim fountain" (see illustration below). This is surrounded by flowerbeds with members of the Arum lily family. Apart from the collection of gentians, the marsh garden, the rose garden, the heather garden and the blue garden, where every possible variety of plant with blue flowers is combined, one of the most striking features is a large lotus pond. The photograph on the right shows part of the formal Italian terraced garden. The central axis is formed by a number of water pools which are at different levels. At the head, just above the waterfall, sits "Il Pescatore," the fisherman's boy, a bronze statue by the Italian sculptor, Gemito (1852-1929).

# HANBURY BOTANICAL GARDEN, LA MORTOLA

The "Temple of the Four Seasons," the neo-classical domed building in the botanical garden at La Mortola is surrounded by succulents, plants which like dry conditions. The trunks of a bottle palm (Nolina beldingii) rise up between the silvery-green leaves of agaves. They are crowned by foliage of narrow, sword-shaped leaves.

# HANBURY BOTANICAL GARDEN, LA MORTOLA

The curiously-shaped purple flowers of Aristolochia hirta, a species of swan flower which is indigenous in the area. ▶

# HANBURY BOTANICAL GARDEN, LA MORTOLA

In 1867, Sir Thomas Hanbury found the perfect spot on the Italian Riviera to establish a garden of exotic plants: La Mortola, near the town of Ventimiglia, on the French-Italian border. The Hanbury Botanical Garden became famous far and wide and is considered to be one of the most important gardens in the Mediterranean area.

# EXOTIC GARDEN, MONACO
(Jardin Exotique)

# EXOTIC GARDEN, MONACO
(Jardin Exotique)

The botanical gardens of the principality of Monaco, "the world's largest rock garden," are unique in Europe. There are gigantic cacti and other succulents growing against the steep slopes of rock formations interlinked by walkways. In other places in Europe these are normally cultivated in conservatories, or at most, placed outside in the summer. Because these fascinating plants are permanently outdoors in the Jardin Exotique, they grow to the same size as they would in their normal habitat over the course of the years. Some old columnar cacti from America grow to enormous heights. Succulents, the collective name for heat-loving plants including cacti, have adapted to the climate of desert areas in a wonderful way. During the short rainy season they store moisture in trunks, roots, branches and leaves. They are found in various parts of the world. Apart from a large number of cacti from America, the succulent Euphorbias, Yuccas, Agaves and Aloes can also be found in Monaco, as well as many small, rare succulents. The Jardin Exotique has developed from 1933 to the present day to become a true paradise for these special plants, not only because of its favorable climatological location, but also because the special requirements of succulents have been met with the help of ingenious artificial means.

-41-

# BOTANICAL GARDENS OF THE VRIJE UNIVERSITY, AMSTERDAM

When the danger of night frost has passed, agaves and furcreas are placed outside the conservatory.

**B**OTANICAL GARDENS OF THE VRIJE UNIVERSITY, AMSTERDAM
Plants such as snakeweed (Echium vulgare), black torch (Verbascum negrum), broad-leaved bell flowers (Campanula latifolia) and Jacob's Cross (Senecio jacobea) flourish in the poor soil of the botanical garden on the site of the Vrije University of Amsterdam.

**B**OTANICAL GARDENS OF THE VRIJE UNIVERSITY, AMSTERDAM
The collection of cacti in the conservatory for succulents. Apart from the cacti, the botanical gardens of the Vrije University also have a large number of other succulents, including many varieties of Sempervivum, with beautiful small rosettes of leaves. The humid atmosphere in the small orchid conservatory is very different from the dry atmosphere in the succulent conservatory, which is cool in winter. In the former there is an impressive collection of Masdevallias from the misty forests of Central and South America. The best conservatory of all is the larger one, with a thriving piece of tropical rainforest, complete with epiphytes, choking plants and creepers.

BOTANICAL GARDENS OF LEIDEN
The new Clusius Garden is a historical monument in the botanical gardens of Leiden, one of the oldest in the world. More than four hundred years ago, a herb garden like this was organized for the University of Leiden by Cluyt, an apothecary from Delft, and Carolus Clusius, a celebrated botanist, who made a great contribution to the spread of the tulip in Europe. Because Clusius had connections everywhere, the garden was well-stocked, not only with the usual medicinal herbs, but with all sorts of unusual plants. Foreign food plants such as melon, tomato and potato were planted, and "garden flowers" such as marigolds and nasturtiums were an added attraction. It was possible to reconstruct the Clusius garden in the botanical gardens in Leiden on the basis of the original inventories dating from that time which had survived.

## BOTANICAL GARDENS OF LEIDEN

On the other side of the pond with its luxuriant vegetation, the elegant hanging branches of the striking old weeping willow can be seen. This has been in the botanical gardens of Leiden since 1840. Apart from the rich and varied collection of plants, which once accounted for the international fame of the botanical gardens in Leiden, it is worth a visit for the peaceful atmosphere and many picturesque spots.

# TROMPENBURG ARBORETUM FOUNDATION, ROTTERDAM

A garden of trees like that at Trompenburg is called an arboretum ("arbor" means tree). The Trompenburg Arboretum was developed in private ownership and still bears the characteristics of the English landscape style used when the garden was planted in 1870. An attempt is made to show the trees in the splendor of all their different forms, especially the oaks, beeches, maples and rhododendrons. As the ornamental value of the garden as a whole is the primary consideration, the arboretum is more of a beautiful area to walk in than an exhibition of trees.

In addition to the approximately 3,000 different varieties of trees and shrubs, the arboretum has also collected perennials and succulents, including Hostas, bamboos (see photograph above: Arundinaria viriditriata), iris, Euphorbia, cacti and small succulents.

# TROMPENBURG ARBORETUM, ROTTERDAM ▶

B OTANICAL GARDENS OF
SALZBURG

B OTANICAL GARDENS OF
SALZBURG

ESTUFA FRIA, LISBON
'Estufa fria' (cold conservatory) is the name of the slatted conservatories which are built against the slope in the Portuguese capital of Lisbon.
Because the natural differences in ground levels have been retained, the vegetation consisting of tropical and subtropical plants forms a beautiful ensemble. The slats provide protection against the sun.

BOTANICAL GARDENS OF THE UNIVERSITY OF COIMBRA

# BOTANICAL GARDENS OF THE UNIVERSITY OF COIMBRA

The hazy green of palm trees, fine-leaved tree ferns, ferns, and various ficus varieties contribute to the special, almost mysterious atmosphere in the heated conservatory of the botanical gardens in Coimbra (Portugal), almost as much as the exotic flowers of the tropical plants.

# BOTANICAL GARDENS, SINGAPORE

Singapore is close to the equator, and under the influence of the very humid, warm climate, it has a rich vegetation which is reflected in the fascinating botanical gardens. Apart from a large number of ornamental tropical, leafy plants, palms and bamboos, flowering orchids can be found in the botanical gardens almost all year round, including the colorful Vanda hybrids with their large flowers (photograph left).

B OTANICAL GARDENS, SINGAPORE

BOTANICAL GARDENS, SINGAPORE
Vanda teres-hybrid (photograph above) and a mixed selection of
orchids (photograph left) in the botanical gardens of Singapore.
The Republic of Singapore has assumed a leading place amongst all
the countries that cultivate orchids in the world because of the
efforts of the botanical gardens in the field of producing hybrids of
orchids. A long time ago the botanical gardens made a name as a
research institute studying useful plants which were imported from
all over the world. In 1877, Singapore first acquired rubber plant
seedlings through the botanical gardens in Kew. When rubber
could be collected from these in about 1890, it proved to be of a very
high quality. Later on, the interest in tropical ornamental plants
became the most important aspect, and the gardens gradually
acquired an idyllic, park-like aspect.

# BOTANICAL GARDENS, SINGAPORE

Leafy plants to a large extent determine the character of the luxuriant vegetation in the botanical gardens of Singapore, and many others in the tropics.  Tall, red variegated plants, such as Cordyline fruticosa "Bella" (syn: C. terminalis) contribute to produce a colorful environment.

BOTANICAL GARDENS, SINGAPORE - NYMPHAEA RUBRA
Like the Victoria, Nymphaea, the water-lily, can be found in virtually all botanical gardens in one or more varieties. The tropical Nymphaea rubra flowers in Singapore. Its dark red, beautifully formed blossoms spread out some distance above the surface of the water. The water plant was originally indigenous in India but has become extremely widespread in many tropical regions. Nymphaea gigantea, which originates from Australia and New Guinea (Irian djaja) is also extremely beautiful. It has fragrant, sky-blue flowers up to one foot wide.

# BOTANICAL GARDENS, SINGAPORE

The phallic flowering spike of Amorphophallus sylvestris rises up from a large purple spadix with a beautifully spreading pleated edge. In the characteristic way of the arum lily family to which this plant belongs, there are male and female flowers on the spadix. The tip is sterile. Apart from Amorphophallus sylvestris, there are approximately eighty other species. One of these, Amorphophallus titanus from Sumatra, has a gigantic spadix more than three feet long. When European botanical gardens successfully get this curiosity to flower in a conservatory, this is recorded in the annals with suitable pride.

BOTANICAL GARDENS, SINGAPORE
The beautiful Traveler's tree (Ravenala madagascariensis) with long-stemmed leaves at the top of the trunk, forming a broad green fan, is an attraction in any tropical botanical gardens. In the botanical gardens of Singapore the vegetation includes a number of specimens. The tree originates from Madagascar. Since the nineteenth century the Traveler's tree has also been imported into Europe, where it is still considered to be one of the most attractive specimens in large palm houses.

ARBORETUM BOTANICKÁ ZAHRADA BRNO
The arboretum and botanical gardens of Brno, a town in
Slovakia (formerly part of Czechoslovakia), date from 1967, and are
therefore still fairly recent.  The botanical gardens are linked to the
university.  They have an area of twenty-five acres with sufficient
space for an arboretum, a steppe landscape, and an alpine garden.
There are special collections of orchids, willows (Salix),
Cotoneasters and alpine plants.

BOTANICAL GARDENS, 'VIERAY CLAVYO,' LAS PALMAS
Like the Jardin Exotique in Monaco, the botanical gardens of Las Palmas on the Canary Islands have a decidedly exotic vegetation by European standards. This group of islands, which belong to Spain, are partly dominated by a tropical or hot climate, and the dry areas are rich in succulents. One of these plants, which have a great propensity for dry conditions is the candelabra-shaped Euphorbia canariensis, which strongly resembles a cactus. Its rectangular pillars rise up high in the landscape. Here, the long stems of Periploca laevigata have twined around the pillars. This climbing plant also likes dry conditions and often finds support on succulent Euphorbias.

BOTANICAL GARDENS, 'VIERAY CLAVYO,' LAS PALMAS
The botanical gardens of Las Palmas have a large collection of plants which are indigenous to the Canary Islands. The photograph shows the large rosettes of leaves of Echium simplex with inflorenscences up to six feet tall. In addition to the indigenous plants, some of the area is devoted to African flora, and many American cacti and members of the bromelia family are represented. The gardens cover an area of sixty acres.

R OYAL BOTANIC GARDENS, KEW
The tops of palm trees and other exotic plants protrude above the elegant wrought-iron spiral staircases and galleries in the Palm House of the Royal Botanic Gardens at Kew. When a palm tree reaches the top of the glass dome, it can develop no further; it is not possible to prune it, because this would also remove the growing tip of the palm.

ROYAL BOTANIC GARDENS, KEW
A flowering Ipomoea acuminata (syn: I. learii), a diurnal flower from tropical America.

ROYAL BOTANIC GARDENS, KEW
The impressive Palm House stands opposite the pond near the Victoria gate entrance of the Royal Botanic Gardens in Kew. This is one of the best known conservatories in the world. It was completed in 1848, a few years after the tax on glass was abolished in England. Instead of the more usual cast iron, the framework was made from wrought iron (the photograph shows a detail of the elegant arched construction). When it was restored, part of the framework was replaced by stainless steel. Although the growth of the tropical plants left a lot to be desired at first, the Palm House immediately attracted the interest of the Victorian public, and the conservatory is still one of the major attractions at Kew.

# ROYAL BOTANIC GARDENS, KEW

It is not for nothing that between a million and a million and a half people visit the Botanical Gardens at Kew, near London every year. Even those who are not directly interested in the scientific aspects can have a wonderful time strolling around the huge estate, enjoying its beauty, the beautiful buildings and the conservatories, the large lake where swamp cypresses are decked in copper-colored leaves in the autumn, the seventeenth century garden behind the Dutch House with a view over the River Thames, the splendid groups of trees and shrubs, and the flowering border plants. The paths lead to a fragrant herb garden, a grass garden, a bamboo garden, a rosarium, and an iris and heather garden. The large rock garden which was planted in 1882 is at its most beautiful in spring, like the rhododendron valley.

# ROYAL BOTANIC GARDENS, KEW

The Royal Botanic Gardens were established in 1759 on the basis of the royal collection of plants of Princess Augusta, the mother of King George III, who lived at Kew House on the Thames, west of London. It was particularly under the supervision of Sir Joseph Banks, the great patron of explorers and plant lovers, that the Botanic Gardens became famous throughout the world. Botanists and collectors were sent to distant lands in every corner of the earth, and had more and more new botanical marvels shipped back to Kew. The strangest structure at Kew, the Pagoda, which is almost 165 feet tall and towers over everything, dates from the age of "chinoiserie," when Chinese architecture and art were all the rage in Europe.

# ROYAL BOTANIC GARDENS, KEW

In the gigantic ten-climate Princess of Wales Conservatory, which was opened by the Princess of Wales in 1987, plants have been brought together which were formerly housed in different conservatories. The conservatory has roofs at different levels, and the foundations are slightly below ground level to prevent cooling off. In contrast with the ornamental Palm House, the designer kept the interior as simple as possible. This means that all the attention is focused on the vegetation, with its specific characteristics in each of the ten distinct climatological zones.

TRESCO ABBEY GARDENS, TRESCO

## TRESCO ABBEY GARDENS, TRESCO

In Tresco Abbey Gardens it is difficult to imagine that one is so close to the predominantly chilly country of England. These botanical gardens are situated on the Scilly Isles, a group of islands in the Atlantic Ocean south of Land's End, which forms the tip of southwest England. The islands were leased by Augustus Smith in 1834. He built a house on Tresco, and had a garden planted. Because of the influence of the warm Gulf Stream, the climate is extremely mild and stable, but the occasional harsh sea winds mean that it is not very suitable for the optimum growth of subtropical plants. Deciduous trees and thick hedges were planted to give protection to the vulnerable plants. It was only when these were fully grown that the garden could develop as a paradise of subtropical plants, where Acacias and Eucalyptus from Australia, succulents from South Africa and cacti from America all feel at home. The Abbey Gardens are still owned by the family.

## DESERT BOTANICAL GARDEN, PHOENIX

The Desert Botanical Garden in Phoenix, Arizona is at its most beautiful in spring, when the majority of desert plants flower, and even the spiniest, apparently almost lifeless cacti produce colorful flowers. The desert garden is devoted not only to desert plants, but also to the lives of humans in arid regions. For example, it shows how the first inhabitants of these regions survived, and reveals how people can live in harmony with the desert.

# DESERT BOTANICAL GARDEN, PHOENIX

More than four thousand different varieties of plants can be found in the botanical garden, covering a huge area surrounded by red rock formations. Half of these are cacti of different shapes and sizes; the rest comprise some of the other intriguing representatives of desert flora. As there are many night-flowering plants, romantic moonlit walks are organized.

# NATIONAL BOTANICAL GARDENS OF SOUTH AFRICA, KIRSTENBOSCH

The flower of the King protea (Protea cynaroides) - known in South Africa as the giant "sugarbush" - has a diameter of approximately one foot. Of the approximately 140 Protea varieties, about a hundred can be found on the coast of the southwest cape in South Africa. When it became clear that the plants were in danger of extinction, the National Botanical Gardens in Kirstenbosch worked hard to cultivate Protea, South Africa's national plant, and spread it. The botanical gardens are situated on the slopes of the Table Mountain near Cape Town, and have specialized in indigenous flora since the beginning of the twentieth century.

◄ NATIONAL BOTANICAL GARDENS OF SOUTH AFRICA, KIRSTENBOSCH

# NATIONAL BOTANICAL GARDENS OF SOUTH AFRICA, KIRSTENBOSCH

Euphorbia ingens, the tree-shaped succulent with many branches, on the left of the narrow path running through the National Botanical Gardens of South Africa, is the most compact representative of the Euphorbia family.

# NATIONAL BOTANICAL GARDENS OF SOUTH AFRICA, KIRSTENBOSCH

Protea nitida, a beautifully formed "sugarbush" in the National Botanical Gardens in Kirstenbosch. Proteas are protected plants in South Africa.

# KAROO NATIONAL BOTANICAL GARDENS, WORCESTER

A flowering Lampranthus and tree-shaped aloes grace
the Karoo Gardens in Worcester (South Africa).

# KAROO NATIONAL BOTANICAL GARDENS, WORCESTER

Apart from the National Botanical Gardens in Kirstenbosch, other botanical gardens in South Africa also carried out research into the conservation of the vegetation in the area. One of these gardens is situated in Worcester in the border area of the Karoo, a region of desert and semi-desert. Botanists from all over the world are intrigued by this area because exceptional succulents grow there. An enthusiast can really indulge himself in this respect in the Karoo

Gardens, which cover an area of 280 acres, of which the majority is reserved for indigenous plants. The profusely flowering Lampranthus is a great attraction. This low-growing shrub is fairly unobtrusive until it starts to flower, when the generally arid valleys are converted into a sea of flowers as if by magic.

## BOTANISKA TRÄDGÄRDEN, GOTHENBURG

The large palm house by the white cast-iron bench was built in 1878, but has been extensively restored since that time. The botanical gardens in Gothenburg, the largest in Sweden, are from a later date. They were planted between 1915 and 1923. The rock garden is particularly special; it contains rare Scandinavian plants which are difficult to grow anywhere else because of their special demands on the environment. They require a cool climate, and in summer they need daylight almost all the day round. The attractive folder invites the visitor to "Travel the world in an hour. Start in Asia !" In fact, the conservatories and the outside gardens contain collections of plants from all over the world. They may not compare with the real Africa, Australia or Asia, but they certainly give an impression of the wealth of the plant kingdom.

◀ BOTANISKA TRÄDGÄRDEN, GOTHENBURG

# INDEX